The Celtic World

You have travelled back in time more than 2500 years to the time of the Celts. They lived in Europe – from Spain in the east to Turkey in the west – from around 750 BC, and spread to Britain from around 600 BC.

Many different groups of people were described as Celts, sharing a common way of life with similar cultures and beliefs. As the Celtic world grew, its languages and customs spread far and wide. We know that the Celts were skilful farmers, talented poets and superb craftsmen and metalworkers. The Celtic people were also well-known for their warlike nature, often fighting and squabbling among themselves.

The Celts reached Britain hundreds of years before the Romans. However, the Romans, like Diodorus Siculus (below), had plenty to say about them.

FOUL FACT! → AROUND 500 BC THE GREEKS CALLED THE PEOPLE OF WHAT IS NOW SOUTHERN FRANCE 'KELTOI'. THE NAME WAS LATER USED TO REFER TO ALL PEOPLE WITH A SIMILAR CULTURE: THE CELTS. EVERYONE WHO MET THE CELTS AGREED THAT THEY WERE TRULY TERRIFYING WARRIORS, WHOSE BITE WAS FAR WORSE THAN THEIR BARK!

DIODORUS HERE! THE KELTOI LOOKED AND SOUNDED TERRIFYING – THEY USED FEW WORDS AND SPOKE IN RIDDLES. THEY LIKED NOTHING MORE THAN BOASTING AND THREATENING PEOPLE, AND YET THEY WERE ALSO QUICK LEARNERS.

FAR AND WIDE
In the 2nd Century BC the Celtic world was at its largest extent (purple). Help these five Celts find their way home by unscrambling their tribe names.

a. lasgu

b. stinalaga

c. renibias

d. eslag

e. tonsrib

Gaels

Britons

Gauls

Iberians

Black Sea

Galatians

Mediterranean Sea

Answers: a. Gauls b. Galatians c. Iberians d. Gaels e. Britons

Society and Laws

The Celts were divided into groups called tribes. Each tribe had a powerful chief or king, who was also its leader in battle. Nobles and warriors made up the highest rank of Celtic society. Below them came druids (priests) and bards (poets). Next were farmers, metal smiths and other workers. At the bottom were slaves.

A KING OR CHIEF HEADED UP EACH TRIBE. A TRIBE WAS MADE UP OF SEVERAL CLANS, AND A CLAN WAS MADE UP OF A CLOSE GROUP OF FAMILIES.

IN CELTIC SOCIETY MEN AND WOMEN WERE TREATED EQUALLY IN MANY ASPECTS OF LIFE, WHICH WAS RARE IN ANCIENT TIMES. WOMEN COULD FIGHT IN BATTLE AND WORK AS CRAFT WORKERS, FARMERS OR DOCTORS, LIKE ME. WOMEN COULD ALSO BECOME DRUIDESSES.

Law and order

Despite the Celts' warlike nature, they had a system of law and order. As learned and highly respected members of society, druids sat as judges. They listened to complaints and quarrels, and decided if a crime had been committed. If it had, they could order a fitting punishment.

What is a tribe without t and e? A RIB!

FOUL FACT! TO DECIDE IF A PERSON WAS GUILTY OF MURDER, THE ACCUSED HAD TO PICK A STICK (WITHOUT LOOKING). IF THEY PICKED THE STICK MARKED 'INNOCENT', THEY WERE FREE TO GO. IF THEY PICKED 'TRINITY', THEY HAD ANOTHER GO. IF THEY PICKED 'GUILTY', THEY WERE PUT TO DEATH.

CRIME AND PUNISHMENT

It was up to the Druid judge to decide on which punishment fitted the crime.
Here are four crimes. Can you match them to the correct punishments?

A. BURNING A HOUSE DOWN

B. RUNNING AWAY IN BATTLE

C. BEATING SOMEONE UP

D. CALLING SOMEONE A NASTY NAME

1. DEATH BY DROWNING IN A SWAMP

2. DEATH BY BEING HANGED FROM A TREE

3. EXILED BY BEING SET ADRIFT IN A BOAT

4. LARGE FINE

CELTS AT WAR

Fearsome Celtic warriors had a reputation for courage and cunning in battle. They liked fighting in single combat, which gave them the chance to show off their bravery. Each side chose a hero to do battle – after they'd traded insults, of course.

CELTIC WARRIORS CHARGED INTO BATTLE NAKED, APART FROM BEING DYED BLUE FROM HEAD TO FOOT! THE DYE CAME FROM A PLANT, CALLED WOAD.

WEAPONS AND ARMOUR

What would a Celtic warrior wear? Use the word list below to number each part of this chieftain's outfit.

1. SHIELD
2. SPEAR
3. IRON SWORD
4. HELMET
5. CHAIN-MAIL SHIRT
6. SLING

FOUL FACT!

THE CELTS LIKED TO CUT OFF THEIR ENEMIES' HEADS AND KEEP THEM AS TROPHIES. WARRIORS SHOWED OFF THEIR PRIZED HEAD COLLECTIONS – THE MORE HEADS YOU HAD, THE BRAVER YOU WERE!

BATTLE FURIES

The Celts had a blood-curdling bunch of war goddesses, called Battle Furies, to watch over them in combat.

MORRIGAN

Morrigan had long red hair and her mouth was on the side of her face. She rode in a chariot pulled by a one-legged horse, and could change her shape to many different animals.

BADBH

Badbh also took the form of a crow, but her tactic was to spread fear and confusion so that warriors came over to her side. Her presence also signified the death of a chief or leader.

MACHA

If a crow was seen before a battle it was a bad sign. Macha turned into this black bird and hovered over the battlefield. She waited to peck at the dead warriors. Macha was also associated with horses.

NEMHAIN

Nemhain (which means 'Frenzy') was goddess of panic and war. She had an ear-splitting shriek, which caused warriors to fall down dead. She is said to have killed 100 men with a single shriek.

FAME GAME

If you wanted popularity and fame you needed to be a Celtic king, queen, warrior, great poet or priest. They were the superstars of the time. Druids had to study for 20 years, which gained them such respect that they didn't have to pay taxes!

YOU KNEW YOU'D MADE IT IF A BARD SANG A SONG ABOUT YOU!

CELTIC HEROES
Meet some Celtic superstars — both legendary and real.

VERCINGETORIX
Chief of the Arverni tribe in France, Vercingetorix led a rebellion against the Romans. He was captured by Julius Caesar, taken to Rome and later executed.

FIONN MAC CUMHAILL
Irish hero Fionn mac Cumhaill gained the world's wisdom when he touched the Salmon of Knowledge. If he needed to know something, he only had to suck his thumb.

CÚ CHULAINN
Legendary Irish hero Cú Chulainn was famous for his superhuman strength. He even battled the monstrous Morrigan, which was no mean feat.

ARTHUR
Arthur is best-known as a legendary British king who led the Knights of the Round Table. However, he appears in Celtic stories as a war leader who fought the Saxons.

The Iceni vs The Romans

One of the most famous Celts was Boudicca, Queen of the Iceni tribe. In AD 60 to 61, she led a rebellion against the Romans. Here are the facts. Who do you think won?

THE ICENI TRIBE

Leader:	Boudicca
Army:	More than 100,000
Weapons:	Spears; swords
Strength:	Fierce fighters; fast charge; hatred of Romans
Weakness:	Lack of discipline

THE ROMANS

Leader:	Gaius Suetonius Paulinus
Army:	Around 10,000
Weapons:	Javelins; shields; swords
Strength:	Organised; disciplined; variety of tactics
Weakness:	Heavily outnumbered

Answer: At first the Iceni had great success, but Boudicca was finally defeated in a bloody battle. Afterwards, Boudicca poisoned herself rather than be captured by the Romans.

Celtic warriors

Instructions

1. Press out all the pieces.
2. Slot a stand into the base of each Celtic warrior to get them ready for battle!

A Celtic chieftain led warriors into battle. He wore a helmet with feathers, wings or a horse's tail attached to it.

Warriors carried long shields in combat, designed with colourful patterns.

Women also fought in battle, the same as men.

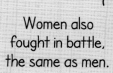

stands

stand

Celtic family

The man was the head of the household, hunting and farming the fields to feed his family.

stands

The woman kept the roundhouse tidy, gathered water and looked after the family's animals.

Children helped out with the jobs at home. Collecting eggs from the chickens was one!

stand

Many boys wanted to be warriors when they grew up. A wooden sword was great for practising combat skills.

stand

Roundhouse

See the following page for instructions.

The Celts built their own family homes, called roundhouses, using materials that were locally available.

The cone-shaped roof was thatched and the walls of the house were wattle and daub — woven branches covered in mud.

wall
(outside)

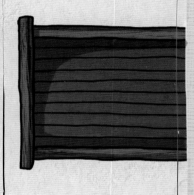

roof
(outside)

wall
(inside)

roof
(inside)

Instructions

1. Press out all the pieces of the roundhouse.

2. To create the circular base, take the two long wall sections. Join the ends by slotting them together, making sure the ends are on the inside. This will help the base hold its shape.

3. To create the cone-shaped roof, join the two roof sections together. Fold the tabs along the creased lines, insert into the slots so the tabs are on the inside. Then unfold the tabs — the two pieces of roof should be joined together securely.

4. Place the roof on the base — your roundhouse is complete! (Take the roof off and look inside to see what a roundhouse was like!)

wall
(outside)

roof
(outside)

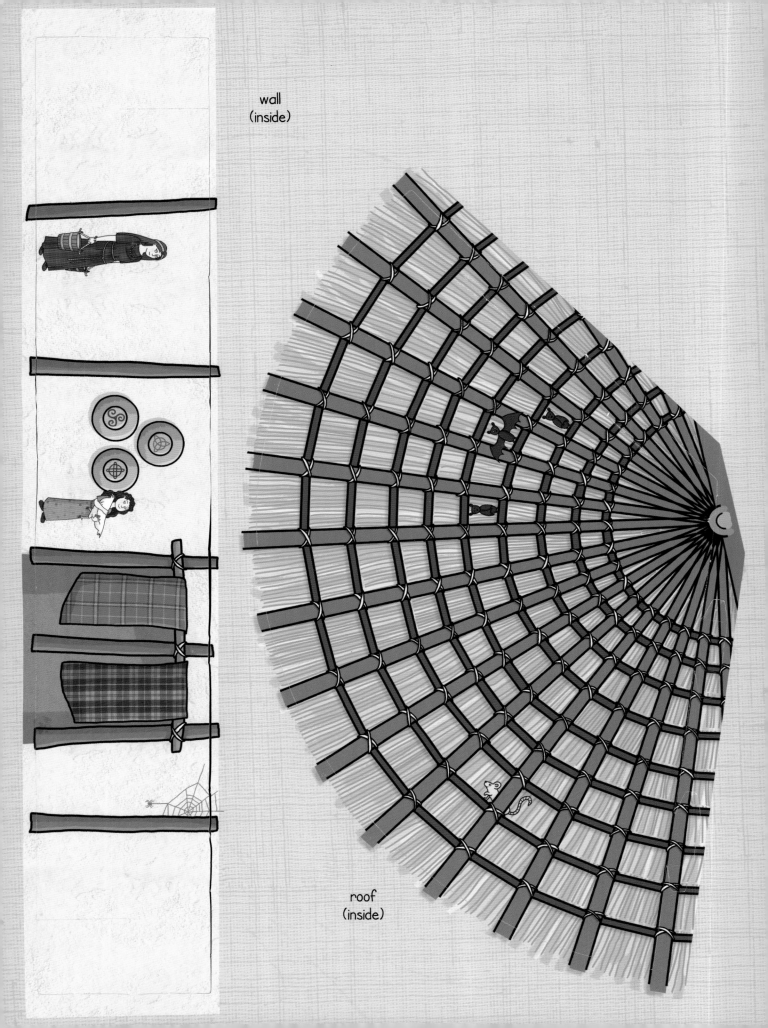

wall
(inside)

roof
(inside)

Celtic shield

The shields of Celtic warriors were boldly coloured and richly decorated. Use the patterns below to decorate your own Celtic shield, or make up your own.

Instructions

1. Press out the shield and the stencil piece.
2. Position the stencil over the shield and use pens or pencils to add a Celtic pattern.
3. Finish the shield by colouring it in.

stencil piece

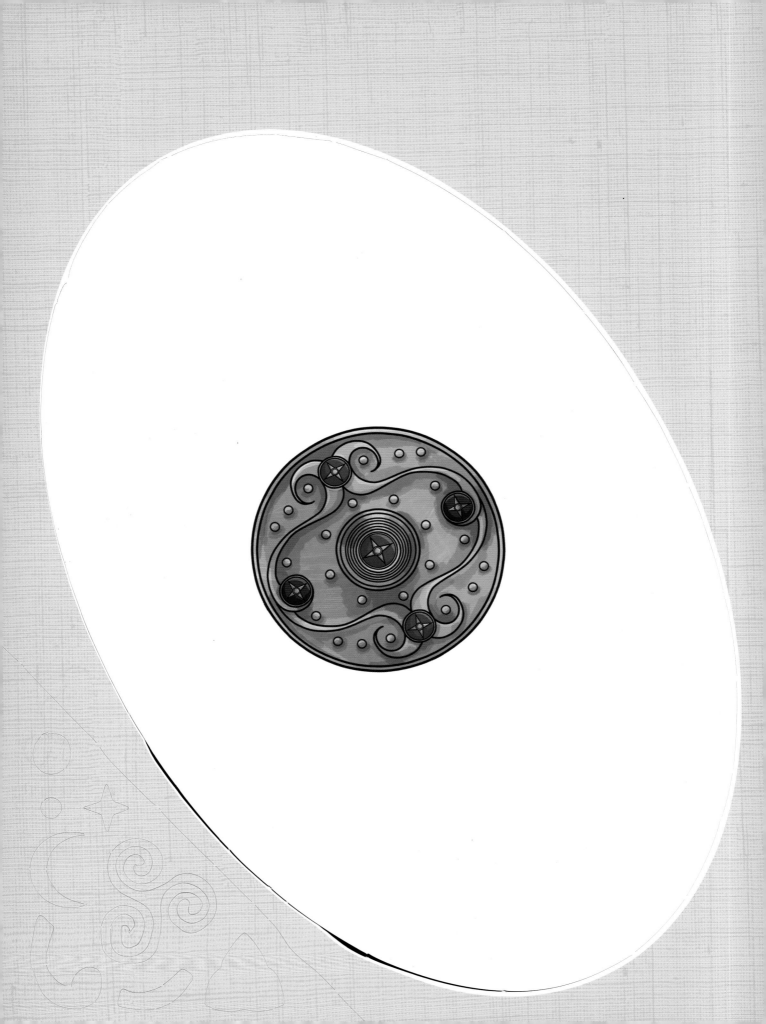

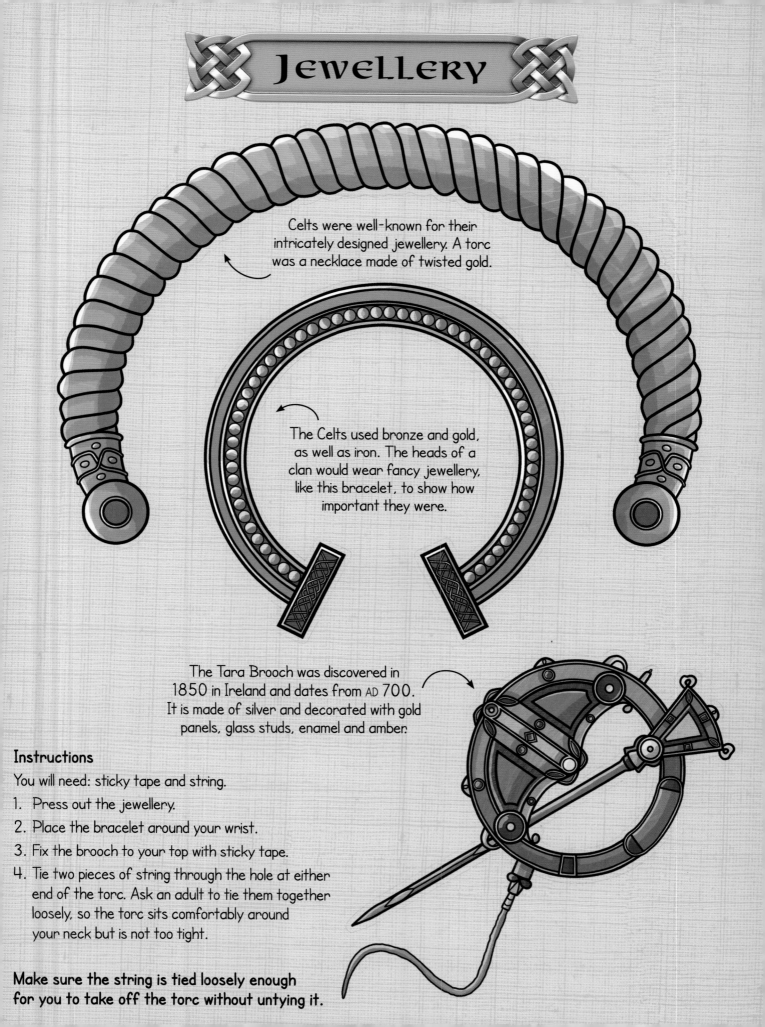

Jewellery

Celts were well-known for their intricately designed jewellery. A torc was a necklace made of twisted gold.

The Celts used bronze and gold, as well as iron. The heads of a clan would wear fancy jewellery, like this bracelet, to show how important they were.

The Tara Brooch was discovered in 1850 in Ireland and dates from AD 700. It is made of silver and decorated with gold panels, glass studs, enamel and amber.

Instructions

You will need: sticky tape and string.

1. Press out the jewellery.
2. Place the bracelet around your wrist.
3. Fix the brooch to your top with sticky tape.
4. Tie two pieces of string through the hole at either end of the torc. Ask an adult to tie them together loosely, so the torc sits comfortably around your neck but is not too tight.

Make sure the string is tied loosely enough for you to take off the torc without untying it.

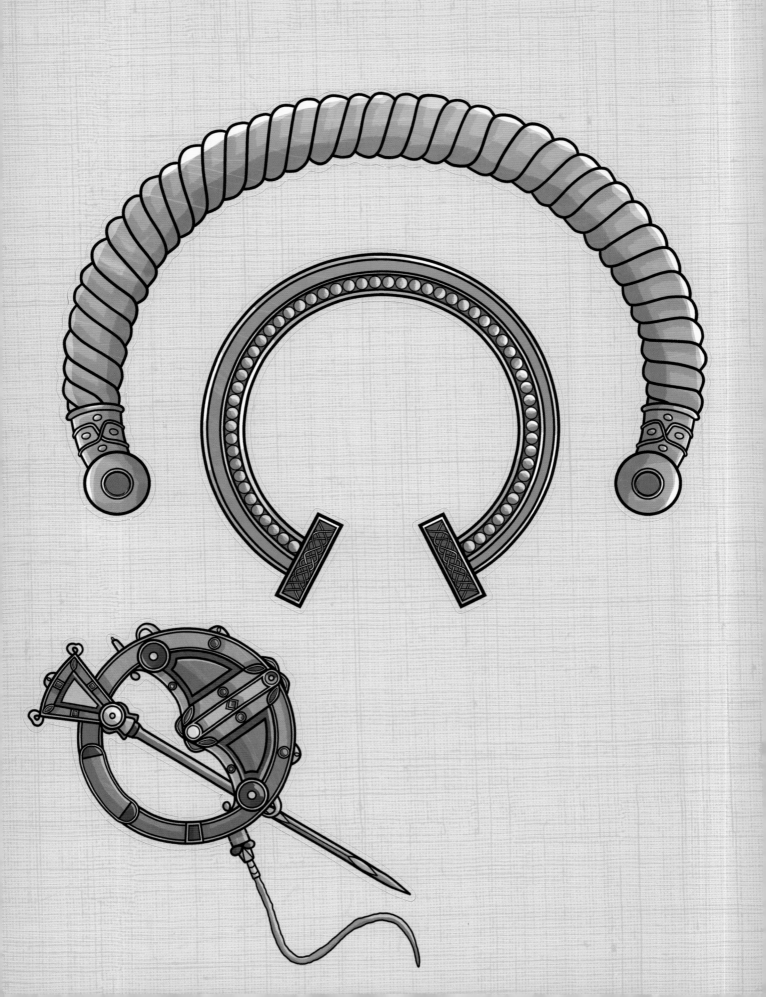

Boudicca

Boudicca, Queen of the Iceni tribe of Eastern Britain, was a brave and fearless leader who destroyed the Roman cities of Londinium (London) and Camulodunum (Colchester).

Instructions

1. Press out the pieces.
2. Slot the stands into the base to make Boudicca's chariot stand.

stands

Celtic gods

Dagda

Brigid

stand

Lugh

stands

Sucellos

CRAFTY CELTS

We know that the Celts were master craftsmen because many ornate items have been discovered from the time. Metal smiths were experts at working bronze and iron into tools, utensils and weapons. They also fashioned silver and gold into beautiful jewellery.

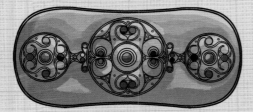

Battersea Shield
Found in the River Thames in 1957, this ornate bronze shield was probably used for ceremonies.

Gold torcs
Many gold torcs have been found. Celtic gods were often shown wearing them — they symbolised wealth, power and courage.

Why did the Celt have a necklace in his mouth? BECAUSE HE TORC'ED TOO MUCH!

BEING A METAL SMITH IN CELTIC TIMES WAS A GREAT JOB TO HAVE! THE CELTS BELIEVED THAT IRON HAD MAGICAL POWERS AND TREATED PEOPLE WHO WORKED IT WITH GREAT RESPECT.

FOUL FACT!
METAL WAS SO PRECIOUS THAT THE CELTS SOMETIMES SACRIFICED THEIR WEAPONS TO THE GODS. THEY THREW THEM INTO LAKES, RIVERS AND BOGS — PLACES THE CELTS THOUGHT OF AS SACRED.

Gundestrup cauldron
Found in 1891 in a bog in Denmark, the cauldron is made of silver and is decorated with detailed scenes.

The spoken art

The Celts loved a good story, especially when it was told by a bard – an official Celtic poet. Bards told tales of heroic deeds, and sang the praises of chiefs and warriors. Becoming a bard took years of training. They had to learn hundreds of poems off by heart and be able to make new ones up on the spot.

CREATE A CELTIC BOWL
The Celts decorated even everyday objects with beautiful, swirling patterns. Use the symbols below to help you decorate your own Celtic bowl.

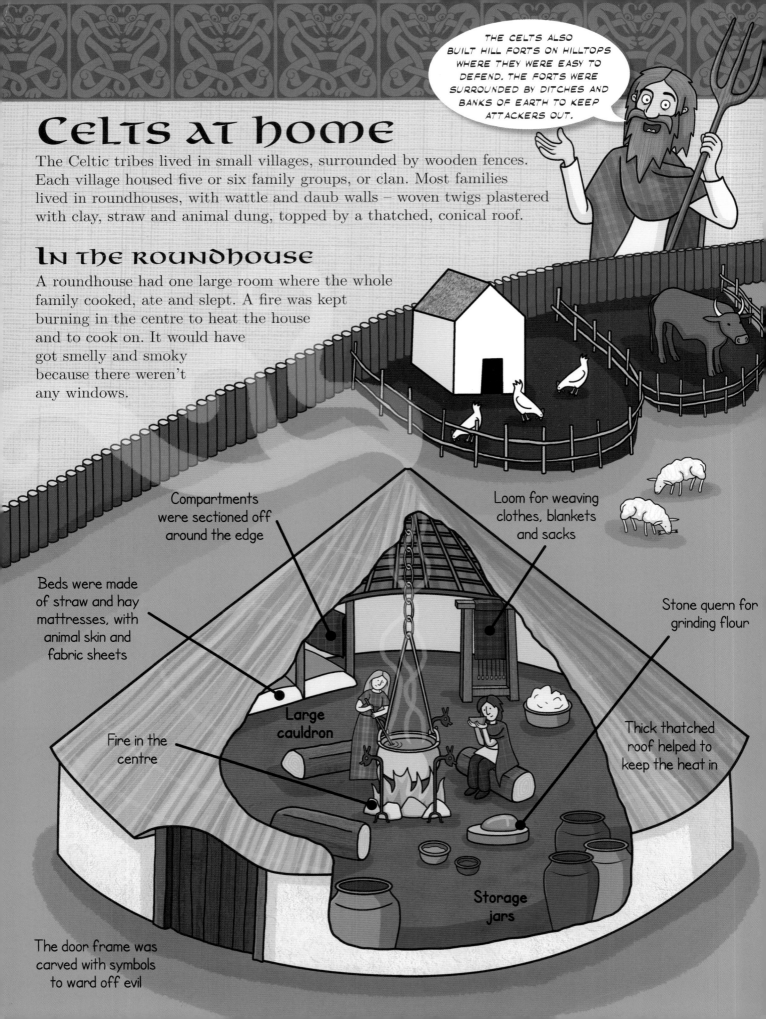

Celts at home

The Celtic tribes lived in small villages, surrounded by wooden fences. Each village housed five or six family groups, or clan. Most families lived in roundhouses, with wattle and daub walls – woven twigs plastered with clay, straw and animal dung, topped by a thatched, conical roof.

In the roundhouse

A roundhouse had one large room where the whole family cooked, ate and slept. A fire was kept burning in the centre to heat the house and to cook on. It would have got smelly and smoky because there weren't any windows.

THE CELTS ALSO BUILT HILL FORTS ON HILLTOPS WHERE THEY WERE EASY TO DEFEND. THE FORTS WERE SURROUNDED BY DITCHES AND BANKS OF EARTH TO KEEP ATTACKERS OUT.

Compartments were sectioned off around the edge

Loom for weaving clothes, blankets and sacks

Beds were made of straw and hay mattresses, with animal skin and fabric sheets

Stone quern for grinding flour

Fire in the centre

Large cauldron

Thick thatched roof helped to keep the heat in

Storage jars

The door frame was carved with symbols to ward off evil

FARMING AND FOOD

Celtic farmers grew crops, such as wheat, barley and beans, in long, narrow fields around their village. They also kept cows, pigs and sheep.

Why did the Celts build roundhouses? BECAUSE THEY WERE SCARED OF CORNERS!

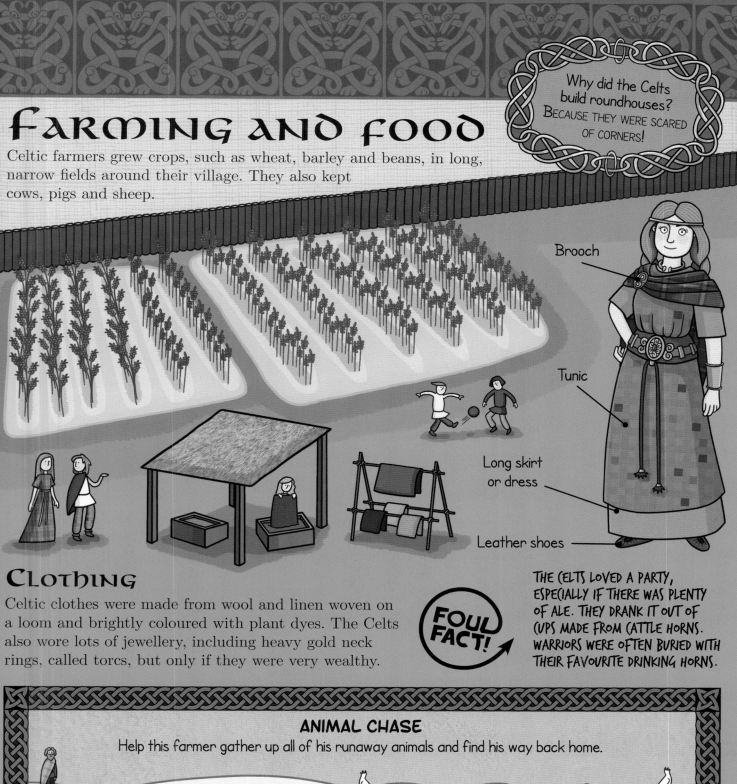

Brooch

Tunic

Long skirt or dress

Leather shoes

Clothing

Celtic clothes were made from wool and linen woven on a loom and brightly coloured with plant dyes. The Celts also wore lots of jewellery, including heavy gold neck rings, called torcs, but only if they were very wealthy.

FOUL FACT!

THE CELTS LOVED A PARTY, ESPECIALLY IF THERE WAS PLENTY OF ALE. THEY DRANK IT OUT OF CUPS MADE FROM CATTLE HORNS. WARRIORS WERE OFTEN BURIED WITH THEIR FAVOURITE DRINKING HORNS.

ANIMAL CHASE
Help this farmer gather up all of his runaway animals and find his way back home.

HOME

GODS AND BELIEFS

Religion was at the heart of everyday life. Celts believed the natural world was full of magic and that many gods and goddesses ruled over it. As well as being judges, doctors and teachers, Druids were the only people who could speak to the gods.

> I AM A DRUID, A PRIEST WHO CARRIED OUT RELIGIOUS CEREMONIES. WE WERE RESPECTED FOR OUR SECRET KNOWLEDGE AND WERE SO IMPORTANT, EVEN CHIEFS HAD TO WAIT FOR US TO SPEAK FIRST.

MEET THE GODS
Meet five of the most powerful gods and goddesses the Celts believed in.

LUGH
God of light and the harvest, Lugh was a skilled warrior. He had a magical spear.

BRIGID
Dagda's daughter and goddess of poetry, medicine and metal.

DAGDA
Father god who protected crops. He owned a magic cauldron filled with never-ending food, and a magical club.

SUCELLOS
God of agriculture and the forest, Sucellos ferried souls to the Underworld. He had a long-handled hammer.

CERNUNNOS
God of fertility, life, animals, forests and the Underworld. He had the antlers of a stag.

FESTIVAL CALENDAR
The Celts celebrated four great festivals through the year, which started on 1 November, to mark the changing seasons.

> LINDOW MAN HERE! I WAS FOUND IN A BOG, WHICH PRESERVED ME VERY WELL INDEED FOR MORE THAN 2000 YEARS. THIS HAS HELPED ARCHAEOLOGISTS TO FIND OUT MORE ABOUT THE CELTS. THEY COULD EVEN TELL WHAT I'D EATEN FOR MY LAST MEAL - BREAD!

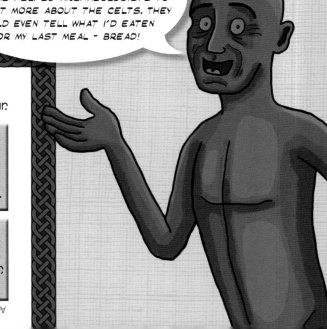

CELTIC FESTIVALS
Number these festivals in the correct order through the Celtic year.

○ **BELTAIN**
The great fire festival of late spring when cattle were left out of their winter quarters.

○ **SAMHAIN**
Marking the start of winter. The dead were believed to return to the land of the living.

○ **LUGHNASA**
A summer festival lasting for a month, to celebrate the harvest.

○ **IMBOLC**
A festival held at lambing time. It celebrated the end of winter, and the goddess, Brigid.

Answers: 1. Samhain (1 November), 2. Imbolc (1 February), 3. Beltain (1 May), 4. Lughnasa (1 August)